The Innocent and Modest Vibiana

DEVOTIONS TO

The Patron Saint of Los Angeles

Presented by Gaudent Angeli

In Remembrance

Of those good men and women who established the One True Faith, and thereby the Mercy of God, in the new world. May they rest in peace. Amen.

Offered For

The renewal of Catholic faith & culture in Los Angeles, California, the Americas, and the world.

Dedication

For Ash, Natalie, and Maria Dolores.

Gaudent Angeli is a 501 (c)(3) nonprofit, and our work is made possible through the generous support of our friends and supporters. We are so grateful for your support in the form of intercessory prayers to our patroness, Saint Vibiana. If you feel called to support our work financially, you may send donations to the address below.

Gaudent Angeli
PO BOX 1015
Claremont, CA 91711

9 781387 720057

TABLE OF CONTENTS

Introduction

"Mind the things that are above, not the things that are upon the earth. For you are dead; and your life is hid with Christ in God. When Christ shall appear, who is your life, then you also shall appear with him in glory."

St. Paul the Apostle,
Colossians 3:2-4

Conventional wisdom tells us that "politics run downstream from culture." This sentiment puts the modern mind's focus on culture as the object of engagement when politics flow amuck, and as the first cause of what we get right or wrong as a society. But culture isn't the fountainhead of the stream, it's just another downstream bend of something more influential that runs above it. What, then, does *culture* run downstream from? The answer is in the word itself: cult (cult•ure).

The word cult is an old word that gets misused and misapplied often in today's vernacular. When post-Christian ears hear it they think of fanaticism or radical religious sectarianism. On the more positive side, in Hollywood, one thinks of cult classic films, with cult followings. Both responses have some truth in the definition they place on cult, but the official, timeless definition is "a system of veneration or religious devotion."

As Catholics, we should welcome this definition, and the word that bears it. In fact, our religion has many cults: the cult of the Saints, the cult of the Sacred Heart, the cult of the Poor Souls, and so on. Cult is a strange word—an other-worldly word, but that's Catholicism. We are in the world, not of it. We are the religion of transubstantiation, relics, uncorrupted mortal remains of Saints, the stigmata, bleeding hosts, and miraculous visions. Our otherworldliness converted whole pagan nations and the entire Roman empire to the One True Faith. Letting go of this strange word (and also our overall strangeness in the eyes of the world) along with its true definition, handicaps our ability to understand and address culture, its issues, its subsequent politics, its politicians and so on.

The culture today in Los Angeles and most of the United States is increasingly anti-Christian and seemingly lost from a Catholic perspective. But it's precisely because we have lost our way in terms of cult that our culture is so wayward. It wasn't always like this.

For over a century, Los Angeles' Catholic cult thrived and influenced the surrounding cultural milieu. Hollywood films were rich in virtue and morals, experiencing a golden age, with many self-proclaimed and devout Catholic actors and actresses. Hard work and duty were held in the greatest regard.

Families were intact. Religion was central to Angeleno life. Cult thrived, and therefore so did culture and everything downhill from it. And it was the cult of St. Vibiana from which L.A. culture flowed.

Gaudent Angeli's thesis is, if we restore the cult of St. Vibiana to what it once was or greater, we will see a renewal of our culture — in the City of Angels, the Americas, and the world.

For the benefit of the reader, therefore, we have assembled a new array of prayers and devotions in honor of St. Vibiana, the patron saint of Los Angeles. May you use them devoutly and grow in fondness, friendship, and dependence on that ancient treasure who laid hidden for nearly 2000 years, only to be unearthed and elevated to the altar of the most populous and visible Catholic Archdiocese in the United States.

About Saint Vibiana

Saint Vibiana was a virgin martyr who
lived and died in third-century Rome.
She lived in a time of great persecution,
when the strong preyed on the weak, and
when many young Christian women were
put to death for rejecting the depravity of
pagan culture. We can be certain of little
about Saint Vibiana's life, except that it
ended with her entrance into Heaven, and
this is the most important thing to know
about any life. After her martyrdom, early
Christians gathered at her tomb to pray
and to remember her great purity. Over
time, however, she was forgotten. In 1853,
her tomb was rediscovered, and her bones
were presented to Blessed Pope Pius IX.
The Holy Father entrusted these relics to
Thaddeus Amat, the soon-to-be Bishop of
Los Angeles. When Bishop Amat arrived in
Los Angeles, the city was a violent frontier
settlement, only recently conquered by

the United States. Amat entrusted the city to Saint Vibiana's patronage, and built a cathedral dedicated to her. Her relics were placed at the main altar. From her position at the heart of the Cathedral, Saint Vibiana watched over generations of Angelenos who came to the Cathedral for baptisms, marriages, funerals, and countless Masses. Her feast day, September 1st, was observed with great reverence and devotion. Today her bones rest in the crypt of Our Lady of the Angels Cathedral, but her soul stands before God, interceding for Los Angeles, and for all those who call upon her name.

For more information, see the section of this book titled "Expanded History," page 101.

1

INNOCENS   ATQUE   PUDICA

V I B I A N A

ORA   ✝   PRO   ✝   NOBIS

Footnotes:

1. This latin invocation comes from the inscription that was found on Saint Vibiana's tomb. The full latin read, literally: "...Innocenti Adque Pudicae Vibiane...." According to our research this was likely "street" latin written by people with only a phoenetic knowledge of the language and not a written knowledge of it. With the help of experts, we took liberties to finess the language into something more representative of proper latin. The invocation here translates "Innocent and Modest [or, pure] Vibiana" and you can find it integrated into a number of the following prayers, as well as themes derived from her name, her virgin-martyr status, and the circumstances of her discovery.

Devotions

ᴜ. Novena

The 1949 Edition,
*Collated and Adapted From
Approved Sources*

Introductory Prayers

† In the name of the Father, and of the Son, and of the Holy Ghost. Amen.

Come, Holy Spirit, fill the hearts of Thy faithful, and kindle in them the fire of Thy love.

V. Send forth Thy Spirit, and they shall be created.
R. And Thou shalt renew the face of the earth.

Act of Contrition

O Jesus Christ, my Lord, true God and true man, I believe and hope in Thee, and I love Thee above all things. Since Thou art infinitely good, I am heartily sorry for having offended Thee. I firmly resolve with the help of Thy grace to sin no more. I beg Thee to grant me the spirit of true devotion, in order that this novena, which

I wish to offer Thee in honor of Saint Vibiana, may invoke her gracious protection and enable me to gain all the indulgences granted to those who perform this holy exercise. Amen.

Prayer to St. Vibiana

O Saint Vibiana, glorious virgin of the Lord, encouraged by thy compassion toward those who have recourse to thee, we present ourselves before thy throne of glory in God's everlasting kingdom, humbly begging thee to hear our prayers and offer them to thy divine Spouse, Jesus. Obtain for us the graces, which we ask in this novena, provided that what we ask pertains to the glory of God, thy honor, and the sanctification of our souls. Amen.

Day

1
~

Meditation on Devotion to St. Vibiana
Reflect, O Christian soul, upon the unfading glory with which heaven has immortalized the name of St. Vibiana. Our Lord assures us that "the just shall shine as the sun in the kingdom of their Father"; and that they "shall be as the angels of God", who continually see the face of their Father in Heaven.

Let us ascend in spirit to the regions of everlasting happiness, and behold our glorious saint in her exalted place among the blessed. There she continually enjoys the possession of that Supreme Good for which we were all created. There she will remain for all eternity. How can we help rejoicing in her glory, ardently desiring to follow in the path of her example, that we may share her happiness for all eternity?

We should also consider her power in favor of those who seek her protection. St. John tells us that "the saints in Heaven shall reign for ever and ever", and that the Lord will give them power over the nations. The saints, being like the angels of God, are also His stewards, sent to minister to them "who shall receive the inheritance of salvation." To this end He commands them to take care of us. He assures us that they rejoice at the sight of a sinner doing penance for his sins. How can we doubt, then, that our holy patroness will surely help us in our difficulties if we earnestly seek her aid?

Prayer to St. Vibiana

Oh, kind and gracious St. Vibiana, we humbly come to thee for help. We know that God will never cast us out, especially if our prayers are offered in union with thine. Intercede for us, that we may be truly sorry for our sins and obtain the grace to lead a good Christian life. We promise to do all in our power to imitate thy virtues, in order that we may deserve thy protection during life and praise and glorify the Divine Majesty with thee throughout eternity. Amen.

O St. Vibiana, pray for us, that our faith may be made strong like thine.
(Our Father, etc. Hail Mary, etc. Glory be to the Father)

O St. Vibiana, pray for us, that our hope may be made confident like thine.
(Our Father, etc. Hail Mary, etc. Glory be to the Father)

O St. Vibiana, pray for us, that our love for God and man may be made pure and ardent like thine.
(Our Father, etc. Hail Mary, etc. Glory be to the Father)

O St. Vibiana, pray for us, that we may loyally profess the Holy Catholic Faith, for

which thou didst cheerfully endure the
pains of martyrdom.
(I believe in God, the Father Almighty, etc.)

Prayer

O St. Vibiana, in thy youth thou didst give
evidence of thy Christian perfection by
despising the world and its illusions in
order to unite thy soul more closely to thy
Spouse, our Lord and Savior Jesus Christ.
For Him did thou endure innumerable
torments and a cruel death. O valiant
martyr of the Lord, thy constancy
proclaims the greatness of thy soul and
the ardent love that filled thy heart. The
sacrifice of thy pure life must ever make thy
prayers acceptable to God. Though we are
poor, miserable sinners, still we confidently
turn to thee, hoping through thine aid to
obtain the graces we ask in this novena,
*(Here let us silently ask the graces and
favors of which we stand in need.)*

We praise and glorify the most holy Trinity,
which on earth adorned thee with the
choicest graces. We also lovingly salute the
spotless Mother of Our Lord, who made
thy torments easier to bear by her sweet
protection. We call upon all the saints in
heaven to pray for us that when our life is
done we may praise, in company with thee,
the Father and the Son and the Holy Ghost
for all eternity. Amen.

Hymn

Come, Holy Ghost, Who ever one
Reignest with Father and with Son,
It is the hour, our souls possess
With Thy full flood of holiness.

Let flesh, and heart, and lips and mind
Sound forth our virtues to mankind;
And love light up our mortal frame
Till others catch the living flame.
Now to the Father, to the Son,
And to the Spirit, Three in One,

Be praise and thanks and glory given
By men on earth, by Saints in heaven.
Amen.

V. O, Saint Vibiana, pray for us.
R. That we may be made worthy of the
promises of Christ.

LET US PRAY

O God, Who amidst other wonders of thine
almighty power hast vouchsafed even to
the daughters of Eve, the grace to gain the
victory of martyrdom; grant, we beseech
thee, that we, who honor the memory of
blessed Vibiana, virgin and martyr, may by
following her example be brought nearer
Thee. Through Jesus Christ our Lord.
Amen.

Day

2

~

Meditation on the Faith of St. Vibiana

Reflect, O Christian soul, upon the generosity of God, Who gave our Saint the priceless gift of faith. From her infancy this virtue was the very life of her soul, inspiring her to dedicate herself entirely to God and to live according to the dictates of our Holy Catholic Faith, Her enemies endeavored to deprive her of this precious gift of God, but neither threats nor flatteries could shake her constancy.

She sealed her profession of faith with her blood, thereby gaining a place in the glorious company of Christ's martyrs. Let us remember that through no merit of our own we have received the gift of faith, without which we cannot please God. Have we always thought, spoken, and acted as faithful children of the Church?

Have we ever been afraid to practice virtue and oppose evil? Perhaps a truthful answer to these questions may embarrass us. Let us beg our Saint to obtain for us the gift of faith, without which we cannot be saved.

Prayer

O Saint Vibiana, valiant martyr, when we think of thy loyal, burning faith and compare it with our own, so weak and tepid, we are ashamed. Take pity on our miserable state, and intercede for us with Christ our Lord. Beg of Him for us the gift of faith, that confessing His name before men, we may be recognized by Him, as His true followers, in the presence of His Father.

Inspired by thy example we finally resolve to conform our lives to the teachings of Christ, to avoid all dangerous company and to be ever zealous for the glory of God and for the honor of our holy Church. Revering the Church as our mother, may we deserve to have God for our Father. Amen.

O St. Vibiana, pray for us, that our faith
may be made strong like thine.
*(Our Father, etc. Hail Mary, etc. Glory be
to the Father)*

O St. Vibiana, pray for us, that our hope
may be made confident like thine.
*(Our Father, etc. Hail Mary, etc. Glory be
to the Father)*

O St. Vibiana, pray for us, that our love for
God and man may be made pure and
ardent like thine.
*(Our Father, etc. Hail Mary, etc. Glory be
to the Father)*

O St. Vibiana, pray for us, that we may
loyally profess the Holy Catholic Faith, for
which thou didst cheerfully endure the
pains of martyrdom.
(I believe in God, the Father Almighty, etc.)

Day

3

Meditation on the Hope of St. Vibiana

Hope is called the anchor of our salvation.
It was this divine virtue that sustained Saint
Vibiana, making her lay hold by
anticipation upon the goods of eternal
life promised by God to His chosen souls.
Hope lead her to look with indifference
upon the perishable things of earth. The
hope of possessing God for all eternity gave
her strength against flatteries, promises
and threats. Fixing her heart on the hope
of heaven's glories, she regarded death as
nothing but the entrance to eternal life.
How different our dispositions are from
those of our Saint!

The infinite mercy of God gives us the
right to hope for the same blessings which
were showered upon her; we have the same
Redeemer who brought her soul to eternal

life. But we forget these things, and only too frequently renounce our hope of eternal happiness in order to devote ourselves to the pursuit of the unsatisfying joys of earth. If we were to think seriously upon these points, we would wonder at our blindness and perversity. We would see how valueless are the things of this life compared with those of eternity.

We would realize that God alone can fill the heart and satisfy the desire for happiness which is a part of our very nature. Let us keep these thoughts in mind, and resolve to imitate our patroness in her contempt for earthly pleasures and her unfailing hope for the imperishable joys of heaven.

Prayer

O Saint Vibiana, thou art for all eternity secure in the possession of God, our Supreme Good. Enlightened by the divine radiance, thy soul can now perceive the glories of the most Holy Trinity, and realize in some degree the greatness of God's love for man. From thy place in heaven look with compassion on us who come to thee. We hope to share thy glory among the saints of God. Obtain for us a ray of heavenly light to guide us through the desert of this world, in order that we may persevere to the end in the service of God, sustained and fortified by Christian faith and hope. Amen.

O St. Vibiana, pray for us, that our faith may be made strong like thine.
(Our Father, etc. Hail Mary, etc. Glory be to the Father)

O St. Vibiana, pray for us, that our hope may be made confident like thine.
(Our Father, etc. Hail Mary, etc. Glory be to the Father)

O St. Vibiana, pray for us, that our love for God and man may be made pure and

ardent like thine.
(Our Father, etc. Hail Mary, etc. Glory be
to the Father)

O St. Vibiana, pray for us, that we may
loyally profess the Holy Catholic Faith, for
which thou didst cheerfully endure the
pains of martyrdom.
(I believe in God, the Father Almighty, etc.)

Day

4

Meditation on the Charity of St. Vibiana

Our Savior says there is no greater love than that which can make a man give his life for his friend. How pure and ardent must have been the love for Jesus Christ which filled St. Vibiana's heart. We can imagine that we hear her say with St. Paul:

"Who shall separate me from the love of Christ? Neither tribulation, anguish, hunger, nor nakedness; neither life nor death, nor things present nor things to come shall ever have the power to part me from my Savior and my God."

How does our lukewarmness compare with St. Vibiana's burning love of God? And yet God loves us, and He gave Himself for us upon the Cross. How coldly indifferent we are to the love of Jesus Christ. Divine love is the mystic fire He came on earth to kindle.

Why does not this heaven-sent flame burn
in our hearts, making us living tabernacles
of divine charity? Our coldness grieves the
Holy Spirit and drives His love far from
us. Let us beg our holy patroness to obtain
for us at least a spark of divine love that we
may learn how sweet it is to love and serve
the Lord our God.

Prayer

O Saint Vibiana, lovely example of true
Christian charity. Our love for God and
man is cold indeed compared with thine.
But we beg thee to obtain for us the grace to
love God truly. In return for this great gift
we promise with God's help to suffer every
torment rather than prove faithless to our
sacred obligations as true followers of Jesus
Christ and members of His Church. Amen.

O St. Vibiana, pray for us, that our faith
may be made strong like thine.
*(Our Father, etc. Hail Mary, etc. Glory be
to the Father)*

O St. Vibiana, pray for us, that our hope
may be made confident like thine.
*(Our Father, etc. Hail Mary, etc. Glory be
to the Father)*

O St. Vibiana, pray for us, that our love for
God and man may be made pure and
ardent like thine.
*(Our Father, etc. Hail Mary, etc. Glory be
to the Father)*

O St. Vibiana, pray for us, that we may
loyally profess the Holy Catholic Faith, for
which thou didst cheerfully endure the
pains of martyrdom.
(I believe in God, the Father Almighty, etc.)

Day

5

Meditation on the Innocence of St. Vibiana

When St. Vibiana's soul had returned to its Creator, the early Christians could think of no other epitaph to place upon her tomb than these words: "To the innocent and pure soul of Vibiana", These few eloquent words, rudely carved on the slab which closed her grave, give testimony that in the minds of those who knew her the glory of her martyrdom was surpassed and, perhaps, eclipsed by the purity which she regarded as her greatest treasure.

She understood that she was born to love and serve God and that she was consecrated to His service by the devout reception of the sacraments. She looked upon herself as a living temple of the Holy Ghost and strove to make herself the worthy tabernacle of so great a quest. The Holy Spirit enriched her with His seven-fold gifts, enabling her to win the palm of martyrdom in early youth. Only He can make us understand what graces He showered upon her. We must remember that by the grace of baptism we too were clothed with the white robe of innocence and made temples of the Holy Ghost. How soon was that white vesture soiled!

The purifying fount of penance is always open to us. Let us once for all resolve to amend our lives. The will of God is our sanctification, and it is only by fulfilling this design of our Creator that our eternal happiness can be assured.

Prayer

O Saint Vibiana, help us to imitate, even though inadequately, thy purity of heart and soul. It was this virtue that made thee dearer to God than did thy glorious martyrdom. We heartily resolve to purify our souls in the precious blood of Christ, by making a sincere confession of our sins. Once in the grace of God, we call on thee to aid us to retain so great a treasure, in order that we may rejoice for all eternity with thee and all the saints in heaven. Amen.

O St. Vibiana, pray for us, that our faith may be made strong like thine.
(Our Father, etc. Hail Mary, etc. Glory be to the Father)

O St. Vibiana, pray for us, that our hope may be made confident like thine.
(Our Father, etc. Hail Mary, etc. Glory be to the Father)

O St. Vibiana, pray for us, that our love for God and man may be made pure and ardent like thine.
(Our Father, etc. Hail Mary, etc. Glory be to the Father)

O St. Vibiana, pray for us, that we may loyally profess the Holy Catholic Faith, for which thou didst cheerfully endure the pains of martyrdom.

(I believe in God, the Father Almighty, etc.)

Day

6

~

Meditation on the Purity of St. Vibiana

It was our Lord's love for the virtue of purity that made Him select a stainless virgin for His Mother. This same love of purity prompted Him to confide His virgin mother to the care of the virgin disciple, St. John, when dying on the cross. Pure souls are the delight of Jesus Christ. He gives them countless blessings and reserves for them in heaven a special glory. Let us reflect a moment on the glory of our patroness in heaven. What joy must fill her soul and how sweet her voice must sound singing the praises of her Lord and God! If we desire to share her happiness and glory, the way is open to us. We must follow her example and turn from everything which may be able to defile our souls. In order to impress upon us the lesson of her purity, the providence of God ordained that on

her tomb these words should be engraved:
"To the innocent and pure soul of Vibiana",
Let us beg for the grace to be made clean
in thought and word and deed. After death,
in company with our saint, we shall then
see the fulfillment of Our Lord's promise:
"Blessed are the pure of heart, for they shall
see God."

Prayer

O Saint Vibiana, virgin bride of jesus Christ
our Lord, we heartily desire to follow thy
example and to share thy glory. We resolve
to practice purity according to our state of
life in all our thoughts and words and acts
from this day forward. We know too well
that we cannot keep this resolution without
a special grace from God.

Pray for us, then, that we may obtain
the grace of purity and thus become fit
dwelling places of the Holy Ghost, and heirs
to the rich blessings promised to the pure
in heart. Amen.

O St. Vibiana, pray for us, that our faith
may be made strong like thine.
*(Our Father, etc. Hail Mary, etc. Glory be
to the Father)*

O St. Vibiana, pray for us, that our hope
may be made confident like thine.
*(Our Father, etc. Hail Mary, etc. Glory be
to the Father)*

O St. Vibiana, pray for us, that our love for
God and man may be made pure and
ardent like thine.
*(Our Father, etc. Hail Mary, etc. Glory be
to the Father)*

O St. Vibiana, pray for us, that we may
loyally profess the Holy Catholic Faith, for

which thou didst cheerfully endure the pains of martyrdom.

(I believe in God, the Father Almighty, etc.)

Day

7

Meditation on the Fortitude of St. Vibiana

The expensive and solid workmanship of St. Vibiana's tomb, compared with the humbler sepulchres around it, lead us to infer that her family was of high position and wealth. Vibiana, as a child, must have been free from every care and accustomed to the comfort of a well-to-do home. A time came, at length, in which she was called upon to sacrifice her faith.

The carefree child became, at once, a valiant woman, braving all the horrors of a cruel martyrdom for the sake of conscience, St. Vibiana's fortitude was based upon her knowledge of her own weakness. She knew that by herself she could do nothing. She had learned that God's grace is necessary in order to do the least of virtuous actions. At the same time she was determined never to renounce her faith. She called upon God for strength to stand the ordeal, knowing that He Who resists the proud is ever ready to confer His grace upon the humble. Her prayer was answered. Heaven-sent grace sustained her through suffering and death. After a few hours of torturing pain, her valiant soul shook itself free from the poor tormented body and flew to receive a crown of everlasting glory. The same God Who sustained our saint will give her followers the same grace of fortitude. Humbly pray for courage to endure the ills of life and to confess our faith with boldness.

Prayer

O valiant martyr, St. Vibiana, wonderful in thy humility and yet more wonderful in thy God-given courage! We need the help of thy prayers. Foolish vanity and groundless pride make our souls cowardly. Beg for us the precious virtue of humility. With this grace we can do all things, for Christ will strengthen us. Fortified by His almighty power, we can endure the sorrows and vexations of our earthly pilgrimage in the blessed certainty that if we bear the cross with patient constancy we shall wear a crown of happiness in heaven. Amen.

O St. Vibiana, pray for us, that our faith may be made strong like thine.
(Our Father, etc. Hail Mary, etc. Glory be to the Father)

O St. Vibiana, pray for us, that our hope may be made confident like thine.
(Our Father, etc. Hail Mary, etc. Glory be to the Father)

O St. Vibiana, pray for us, that our love for God and man may be made pure and ardent like thine.
(Our Father, etc. Hail Mary, etc. Glory be to the Father)

O St. Vibiana, pray for us, that we may loyally profess the Holy Catholic Faith, for which thou didst cheerfully endure the pains of martyrdom.

(I believe in God, the Father Almighty, etc.)

Day

8

~

Meditation on the Protection of St. Vibiana
Nothing happens by chance. It was by a
special design of Providence that St.
Vibiana's body found its way to this coast,
so far away from its first resting-place
and fifteen centuries after her death. The
circumstances all lead us to believe that
from eternity the Lord had destined St.
Vibiana to be the guardian angel of the
Church in Southern California.

The Vicar of Christ placed us and our
interests, both spiritual and temporal,
under the protection of this virgin-martyr.
We have no right to fear that she will fail
in the performance of her sacred trust. We
must do our part; she will never be found
wanting. What must we do to obtain the
benefit of St. Vibiana's protection? First
of all, we must imitate her virtues—her

faith, her purity, her courage—carefully avoiding everything which may hurt our faith, stain our souls, or weaken our sense of duty. Second, we should pray to her with devotion and place ourselves under her protection. Lastly, we must try to spread devotion to her among our friends and acquaintances.

In all our difficulties we should go to her with confidence and we should praise the providence of God, which has given us the grace of having her for our special advocate before His throne of mercy. Let us resolve to receive the sacraments frequently and worthily, striving constantly to uproot all evil from our hearts and habits. Thus we pave the way for God's indwelling grace which alone can make us true and perfect Christians.

Prayer

O Saint Vibiana, our beloved patroness, receive us beneath the mantle of thy kind protection and obtain for us the grace to be as truly thine as thou art truly ours. With the help of God and the assistance of thy prayers we promise to make every effort to imitate thy virtues in the hope that we may share thy glory in the mansions of eternity. Amen.

O St. Vibiana, pray for us, that our faith may be made strong like thine.
(Our Father, etc. Hail Mary, etc. Glory be to the Father)

O St. Vibiana, pray for us, that our hope may be made confident like thine.
(Our Father, etc. Hail Mary, etc. Glory be to the Father)

O St. Vibiana, pray for us, that our love for God and man may be made pure and ardent like thine.
(Our Father, etc. Hail Mary, etc. Glory be to the Father)

O St. Vibiana, pray for us, that we may loyally profess the Holy Catholic Faith, for which thou didst cheerfully endure the pains of martyrdom.
(I believe in God, the Father Almighty, etc.)

Day

9

**Meditation on the Consecration of
Ourselves to St. Vibiana**

There are several reasons why we should
devote and consecrate ourselves in a special
manner to St. Vibiana.

First, by so doing we shall be acting in
accordance with the manifest will of God
by Whose Providence we have been placed
under her protection.

Second, it is the desire of the Church,
indicated by the Holy Father's presentation
of the sacred body of our Saint to the
Cathedral of this Archdiocese.

Third, the Saint herself is anxious to carry
out the designs of Divine Providence in
making her our advocate and patroness.

Last of all, our soul's best interests will be advanced if we confide them to her hands.

The advantages of this consecration of ourselves to the loyal service of our patroness are many and great. In the first place, our prayers will reach heaven in union with hers. Second, she will take care of our necessities of soul and body, she will protect us in the time of danger, guide us in doubts and perplexities, comfort us in afflictions, and strengthen us in the hour of temptation. She will be our consolation during sickness, and in death our strong defense against the powers of darkness.

Finally, when our souls leave this earth she will present them at the judgment seat of Christ to plead our cause. Let us resolve to confirm our consecration to St. Vibiana by following her example. Living as true followers of Jesus Christ should live, we may hope to depart this life in peace and after death to sing the praises of the Father

and of the Son and of the Holy Ghost
through all the endless ages of eternity.

Act of Consecration to
Saint Vibiana

O Saint Vibiana, our most loving and
beloved patroness, in thy early childhood
thou didst consecrate thyself to God. We
now intend to follow thy example and
devote ourselves entirely to Him. We place
our souls in thy pure hands, and beg thee to
present them at the throne of grace.

By thus entrusting our most sacred interests
to thy safekeeping, we are sure that we will
be made more acceptable to God. In holy
baptism we were dedicated to His service,
offering our bodies and our souls, our
very life itself entirely to Him. Beside the
baptismal font we solemnly renounced the
world, the devil and the flesh with all their
vain deceits; there we promised to spend
our lives in the sweet service of our Saviour

and our God. But how poorly we have kept our word!

Here, before His altar we humbly acknowledge our numerous transgressions and are truly sorry for them. Knowing that His grace is given only to the humble, we prostrate ourselves in soul and body at His sacred feet and beg of Him, through thy intercession, strength to live up to our Christian obligations.

We renew our consecration to God, and, after God, to thee. We promise faithfully to imitate thy virtues. Help us to keep this resolution. Receive us under thy protection as thy special charge, given to thee by the Providence of God. We earnestly beseech thee not to leave us until with thee we meet before the throne of God to offer Him our everlasting gratitude for granting us eternal happiness in answer to thy prayers. Amen.

O St. Vibiana, pray for us, that our faith
may be made strong like thine.
*(Our Father, etc. Hail Mary, etc. Glory be
to the Father)*

O St. Vibiana, pray for us, that our hope
may be made confident like thine.
*(Our Father, etc. Hail Mary, etc. Glory be
to the Father)*

O St. Vibiana, pray for us, that our love for
God and man may be made pure and
ardent like thine.
*(Our Father, etc. Hail Mary, etc. Glory be
to the Father)*

O St. Vibiana, pray for us, that we may
loyally profess the Holy Catholic Faith, for
which thou didst cheerfully endure the
pains of martyrdom.
(I believe in God, the Father Almighty, etc.)

ɪɪ. Prayers for
the Laity

For a Petition

God Most Great, Thou chose the weak of this world to confound the strong. Through the intercession of the patroness of the Archdiocese of Los Angeles, the most innocent and modest Vibiana, virgin and martyr, deign to grant me the favor of...

(Here make your petition).

Amen.

For Families

Most innocent and modest Vibiana, patroness of the Archdiocese of Los Angeles, you found everlasting life in the Living One by glorifying God Most Great in thy chaste obedience as virgin and martyr. Through thy intercession we pray for faithful, fruitful families devoted to the Lord in this life so that we may adore Him with thee forever in the life to come. Amen.

For Faithful Laity in LA I

Most innocent and modest Vibiana, you
are a living stone, rejected indeed by men,
but chosen and made honourable by God;
under thy patronage build up for us in
the Archdiocese of Los Angeles a spiritual
house, a holy priesthood, of sons and
daughters offering up spiritual sacrifices
acceptable to God Most Great through Jesus
Christ our Lord. Amen.

For Faithful Laity in LA II

Most innocent and modest Vibiana,
patroness of the Archdiocese of Los
Angeles, doubly crowned with the white
rose of virginity and the red rose of
martyrdom, you reigneth now forever with
Jesus Christ our Lord. May we follow thy
constancy in the faith in this present age
and so behold things eternal. Through God
Most Great. Amen.

For Faithful Laity in LA III

God Most Great, in Thy servant, the innocent and modest Vibiana, Thou joined the flower of virginity with the palm of martyrdom. Be pleased, by her intercession as patroness of the Archdiocese of Los Angeles, that we may abide in the true vine, remaining clean as she did, and bearing much fruit to the glory of the Father. Amen.

For Faithful Laity in LA IV

Most innocent and modest Vibiana, patroness of the Archdiocese of Los Angeles, you refused to sacrifice the spotless flower of chastity in the face of persecution for the Holy Name of Jesus, thus winning with it the fragrant palm of martyrdom. Intercede for us, we pray, and so win for us the graces we need to overcome the confusions and hostility of this world so that we too may find life everlasting. We ask this through God Most Great. Amen.

III. Prayers for the Clergy & Religious

SANTA BARBARA MISSION CHOIR LOFT

For Priests

Most innocent and modest Vibiana,
esteemed worthy of the double honour
of virginity and martyrdom, we implore
thee as patroness of the Archdiocese of Los
Angeles to grant us faithful priests, clothed
with holiness before God Most Great.
Amen.

For Religious

Most innocent and modest Vibiana, virgin
and martyr, you became a sacrificial
offering pleasing to the Lord; we implore
thee as patroness of the Archdiocese of
Los Angeles to grant us faithful men and
women who will answer the summons of
God Most Great and serve His Holy Church
in poverty, obedience, and chastity. Amen.

IV. Prayers for Pastors & Governors

Los Angeles Court House

For Bishops

God Most Great, who hath by Thy Holy
Spirit placed bishops to rule Thy Church,
through the intercession of the patroness
of the Archdiocese of Los Angeles, the most
innocent and modest Vibiana, virgin and
martyr, deign to grant us blameless bishops
and faithful shepherds to teach, govern, and
sanctify Thy people. Amen

For Governors

God Most Great, to Whom all powers
of the earth are answerable, through
the intercession of the patroness of the
Archdiocese of Los Angeles, the most
innocent and modest Vibiana, virgin and
martyr, deign to grant us faithful servants
to govern the people of this land in
accordance with Thy holy will. Amen.

v. Prayers for the Cult of Vibiana

St. Vibiana Cathedral

I

God Most Great, who madest Thy servant,
the most innocent and modest Vibiana, a
spotless virgin, a holy martyr, a living one
in whom Thou livest, we beseech Thee
that devotion to her name and her cult
may spread throughout the Archdiocese
of Los Angeles, renewing us in faith and
conforming us through her example and
prayers to Thy Son, our Lord and Savior
Jesus Christ, under the protection of Our
Lady, Queen of the Angels. Amen.

II

God Most Great, Who madest Thy servant
blessed Vibiana, by her virginal purity and
sacrificial death, an icon of Thy Son, Jesus
Christ, our Lord, grant, we humbly implore
Thee, that all who honour her as patroness
may be helped by the splendor of her
merits of chastity and fortitude so pleasing
to Thee, so that our dutiful service may find

favor in Thy sight and obtain from Thee the grace of victory for us, under the protection of Our Lady, Queen of the Angels. Amen.

A Litany

Lord, have mercy on us

Christ, have mercy on us

Lord, have mercy on us

Christ, hear us

Christ, graciously hear us

God the Father of heaven, have mercy on us

God, the Son, the Redeemer of the world, have mercy on us

God, the Holy Spirit, have mercy on us

Holy Trinity, one God, have mercy on us

Holy Mary, pray for us

Holy Mother of God, pray for us

Holy Virgin of virgins, pray for us

Most innocent and modest Vibiana, pray for us

St. Vibiana, virgin daughter of the Church,
pray for us

St. Vibiana, pleasing to the Lord,
pray for us
St. Vibiana, presented as a chaste virgin to
Christ, pray for us
St. Vibiana, clothed in fine linen,
pray for us
St. Vibiana, who arose and trimmed her
lamp, pray for us
St. Vibiana, who went out to meet the
Bridegroom and the bride,
pray for us
St. Vibiana, over whom the Bridegroom
rejoiceth, pray for us
St. Vibiana, following the Lamb
whithersoever he goeth, pray for us
St. Vibiana, making merry with timbrel and
dancing, pray for us
St. Vibiana, coming with joyfulness,
carrying her sheaves, pray for us

St. Vibiana, tested and found worthy,
pray for us
St. Vibiana, gold in the furnace,
pray for us
St. Vibiana, unashamed of Christ,
pray for us
St. Vibiana, who sought the Lord and his
strength, pray for us
St. Vibiana, persecuted for righteousness's
sake, pray for us
St. Vibiana, killed in body but not in soul,
pray for us
St. Vibiana, poured out like a libation,
pray for us
St. Vibiana, who endured to eternal life,
pray for us
St. Vibiana, in the hand of God,
pray for us
St. Vibiana, abiding with Him in love,
pray for us

St. Vibiana, seed for His vineyard,
pray for us

St. Vibiana, vintage of His vineyard,
pray for us
St. Vibiana, whose vine has brought forth a
pleasant aroma, pray for us
St. Vibiana, whose flowers are ready to
bring forth fruit, pray for us
St. Vibiana, precious fruit of the earth for
whom the husbandman waited,
pray for us
St. Vibiana, dwelling in the land of the
living, pray for us
St. Vibiana, a living stone, chosen and made
honourable by God,
pray for us
St. Vibiana, child of the ever-living God,
pray for us
St. Vibiana, temple of the living God,
pray for us

St. Vibiana, rejoicing in the living God,
pray for us

Lamb of God, you take away the sins of the world,

Spare us, Lord.

Lamb of God, you take away the sins of the world,

Graciously hear us, O Lord.

Lamb of God, you take away the sins of the world,

Have mercy on us.

V. Behold, now she follows the Lamb who was crucified for us,
R. powerful in virginity, modesty her offering, a sacrifice on the altar of chastity

Let us pray:
God Most Great, who in the midst
of pagan Rome, bestowed upon Thy
innocent and modest daughter Vibiana the
twofold incorruptible crown of virginity
and martyrdom, teach us through her
intercession to imitate her purity and
to offer ourselves in sacrifice, under the
protection of our Lady, Queen of the
Angels, through Jesus Christ our Lord.
Amen.

VI. Prayers to the Mission Saints of Los Angeles

Celebrating the 250th Anniversary of the Mission San Gabriel

Prayer to St. Junipero Serra

Blessed Junipero Serra, our patron, you humbly spent yourself to build up the Church as the Apostle to California, intercede for the Archdiocese of Los Angeles, we pray, especially for our holy priests and religious, that we too may go always forward in service to our Lord Jesus Christ.

Amen.

Prayer to St. Ferdinand

Blessed Ferdinand, our patron, by your holy example of devoted service and stewardship, intercede for the Archdiocese of Los Angeles, we pray, protecting and purifying our public life and strengthening our families to withstand and overcome every enemy of the true faith.

Amen.

Prayer to St. Barbara

Blessed Barbara, our patron, venerated throughout east and west for your purity and sacrifice as one of the Holy Helpers of the Church, intercede for the Archdiocese of Los Angeles, we pray, that we may always be shielded from every harm and blossom in attentive wonder toward God's creation.

Amen.

Prayer to St. Bonaventure

O God, Who gave to Your people blessed Bonaventure as a minister of salvation, grant, we beseech You, that we who cherished him on earth as a teacher of life, may be found worthy to have him as an intercessor in heaven.

Amen.

Prayer to St. Agnes

Blessed Agnes, our patron, as a faithful spouse to Christ Jesus and a gentle lamb upon the altar of sacrifice, intercede for the Archdiocese of Los Angeles, we pray, and especially for the youth of our diocese, that we too may grow in chaste love and faithful devotion.

Amen.

Prayer to St. Gabriel

Holy Gabriel, our patron, you were appointed guardian of Israel and herald of the Messiah, protect and intercede for the Archdiocese of Los Angeles, we pray, that we too may have God for our strength and may joyfully announce the lordship of Jesus Christ.

Amen.

Prayer to the Immaculate Conception

O God, Who, by the Immaculate Conception of the Virgin, didst prepare a worthy habitation for Thy Son, we beseech Thee, that as by the foreseen death of that same Son, Thou didst preserve her from all stain, so too thou wouldst permit us, purified through her intercession, to come unto Thee. Through the same Christ our Lord. Amen.

Amen.

More About
St. Vibiana

VII.
Expanded
History

"Barely had it reached the high seas when it seemed as though all the furies of the lower world had conspired to prevent the sacred relic from entering the diocese in which it was destined to be enshrined."

– Account of the voyage of St. Vibiana's relics to the California coast.

Timeline of Devotion

On December 9, 1853, the anniversary
of the first apparitions of Our Lady of
Guadalupe in Mexico, archeologists
excavating the newly-found Roman
Catacomb of Pope Sixtus (Pretestato)
discovered a burial vault closed with a
marble slab that read in Latin: "To the
soul of the innocent and pure [or, modest]
Vibiana, [laid to rest] in peace a day before
the September Calends" (i.e. on the eve
of September 1st). The inscription was
concluded with a drawing of a laurel wreath,
believed to be an early Christian symbol
of martyrdom. Next to the sepulcher, a
rose-colored crystal vial was found. At
once the discovery was related to the
religious authorities and since the name of
Vibiana was not mentioned in any Roman
Martyrologies (not to be confused with
the 4th century martyr Bibiana), Blessed
Pope Pius IX ordered an investigation. The
appointed commission had established that

the skeleton belonged to a young woman apparently put to death in a violent fashion. The writings on the neighboring epitaphs suggested that the burial took place in the third century. The crystal flask was thought to contain the martyr's blood, which according to some reports had not lost its reddish hue, and seemed to complement the wreath symbol.

Vibiana was proclaimed a saint and thousands of faithful rushed to Rome in February of 1854 to venerate the tomb of the newly-manifested virgin-martyr. Various Bishops petitioned the pope for the custody of the sarcophagus, but it was the newly consecrated Bishop Thaddeus Amat of Monterey that received the relics with a provision that a cathedral be built in honor of this saint in California. In December 1855, after a long and tumultuous sea voyage, the saint's remains came to Santa Barbara. Early the next year, the Holy See declared Vibiana a principal patroness of the Monterey Diocese with her feast set for September 1st and accompanied by the publication of the first Novena.

In the summer of 1863, an apparent miracle had taken place: the fire that had broken out and consumed the entire Church of Our Lady of Sorrows in Santa Barbara had not touched the relics of Vibiana. Although the glass sides of the case were cracked and blacked by fire, the wax effigy and silken robes that encompassed the relics somehow remained untouched.

In 1868 the relics were moved to a growing city called Los Angeles (originally deposited in the Old Plaza Church), and finally they were solemnly enshrined above the high altar of the newly built St. Vibiana Cathedral (April 1876) with thousands of Angelenos in attendance. Only then did the aging Bishop Amat remember the dream he saw as a seminarian of a young woman who told him that one day he would build a cathedral in her honor...

Conclusion

And thus, for the next 100 years St. Vibiana was venerated, revered, and treasured by the faithful in Southern California as a beloved patroness.

Hidden from sight and almost forgotten, Vibiana is remembered and considered a saint to this day by many generations of Angelenos. The faithful unite to form organizations and movements to prayerfully ask their patron for intercessions; pilgrims and guests of the city come before the tomb to pay their respects to a regional saint and even the local Eastern Orthodox stop by once in a while to honor the relics of the early Church's martyr. The memories of her diocesan patronage, the miraculous transport and preservation of her relics, the dedication of her cathedral and her apparition to a young Bishop Amat keep the candle of public devotion lit amidst a modest historical record of her life and death.

While at this time there may be no scientific or documentary proof to verify how she died or what kind of life she lived, the faithful continue to venerate her as a paragon of modesty, purity, innocence, and courageous faith in the face of persecution.

Perhaps it is through you, dear reader, and our joint prayers that God Most Great will, as often is the case, reveal the glory of His saints.

To Him be victory, glory and empire now and forever. Amen.

*The following letter was written by
Bishop Thaddeus Amat to the faithful of
Los Angeles, announcing the establishing
of the "Association of St. Vibiana" by
Blessed Pius IX (a sodality/confraternity
of lay faithful to promote and fund the
building of the Cathedral in her name).
Although it no longer exists as an official
institution of the Church, we wish to share
this piece of history which was published
in the 'Centennial History' of St. Vibiana
Cathedral by Msgr. Francis J. Weber in
1976, to show how interested Blessed Pius
IX was in the future flourishing of our great
archdiocese.*

The Association of St. Vibiana

Having the Holy Father, Pius IX, given to the Diocese of Monterey and Los Angeles, California, at the request of its Bishop, the precious body of Saint Vibiana, and appointed the same as Patroness of said Diocese, with the express condition of building the Cathedral Church in honor of the Saint: the Bishop anxious to carry out the object of His Holiness in erecting the building, the want of which is already felt, without weighing heavy upon his faithful, on the contrary with advantage even to the poorest, established an Association in his Diocese, by which the members thereof, by contributing the small sum of 12 1/2 cents per month for a certain space of time, calculated at about 20 years to complete the work, would be entitled to the honors of " Benefactors of the Church," and as such would have a share in the Holy Sacrifice of the Mass offered up for them every first day of each month, unless it be a festival day, in which case it is offered up the next morning, and would partake of the suffrages which will be made for the Benefactors of the Church, when it shall be built.

The Holy Pontiff, Pius IX solicitous also to see the Cathedral in honor of the Patron Saint finished, by His Apostolic Breef *Ad perpetuam rei memoriam*, dated Rome, January 7th, 1859, approved said Association, raised it to the rank of a regular Confraternity or Sodality, and granted to all and each of its members of both sexes in any part of the world, to all the Faithful of Jesus Christ, the following Indulgences.

I.

Plenary Indulgence on the day of their entering said Association, provided that being truly penitent they go to Confession and receive the holy Communion.

II.

Plenary Indulgence in the article of death, if truly penitent having confessed and received the holy Communion; or in case they could not, at least being contrite, they pronounce devoutly, with their heart, if they cannot with their mouth, the holy name of "Jesus."

III.

Plenary Indulgence to be gained on the day of Saint Vibiana (1st of September) or on any of the seven following days that they would select, provided that being truly penitent and having confessed and received the holy Communion, visit the Church of Saint Vibiana when it will be built, or their own parochial Church, praying to God for peace amongst the Christian Princes, for the extirpation of heresies and the exaltation of our holy mother the Church.

IV.

Plenary Indulgence and the remission
of all sins once a month on any day
they may select, if truly penitent and
having confessed and received the holy
Communion, visit the Church and pray, as
above.

V.

One hundred days Indulgence for every
good work which they shall perform, at
least with a contrite heart.

VI.

He declares all these Indulgences applicable
to the souls in Purgatory.

VII.

Finally, He grants the favor of a "Privileged
Altar" to that on which the precious body
of Saint Vibiana shall be deposited, and for
all the Masses which shall be celebrated
thereon.

All this "notwithstanding whatever Decree to the contrary."

All persons wishing to join this Association and partake in all the favors herein specified, may do so by paying their full subscription at once, $30, and their names shall be entered amongst the members and Benefactors.